Pearl Harbor Child

A Child's View of Pearl Harbor —
from Attack to Peace

by
Dorinda Makanaōnalani
Stagner Nicholson

designed and edited by
Larry Nicholson

60th Anniversary Edition
Copyright © 2001 Dorinda M. Nicholson, all rights reserved.

Concept and design by Larry Nicholson
Published by Woodson House Publishing P.O.Box 16536 Kansas City, MO 64133
     Phone: 800-555-2693 Email: larry@pearlharborchild.com
     Web Site: www.pearlharborchild.com

     First Printing, 1993
     Second Printing, 1994
     Third Printing, 1995
     Fourth Printing, 1998
     Fifth Printing, 2000
     Revised and expanded edition, First Printing, March, 2001

Summary
     Dorinda Nicholson, a primary source, tells her personal account of witnessing the bombing of Pearl Harbor and the events that followed, including blackouts, rationing, air raid drills, gas masks, censorship, martial law, wartime currency, and finally, peace. Her unique experience is enjoyable reading for all ages, telling the story from a civilian point of view, written by a woman, through the eyes of a child.

Library of Congress Cataloging-in-Publication Data

     Library of Congress Control Number: 2001088430
Nicholson, Dorinda Makanaonalani
     Pearl Harbor Child: a Child's View of Pearl Harbor—from Attack to Peace
     by Dorinda Makanaonalani Nicholson; designed/edited by Larry Nicholson
     90p., ill., map, ports.; 20 x 24 cm.
     ISBN 0-931503-02-7
     1. [Pearl Harbor (Hawaii), Attack on, 1941 -- Personal narratives]
     2. [World War, 1939-1945 -- Hawaii]
     3. [World War, 1939-1945 -- Personal narratives, American]
     940.53/nic -- dc21
     D744.7.H3 N5 1993

Originally published by Arizona Memorial Museum Association, Honolulu, HI
Current edition published by Woodson House Publishing, Kansas City, MO USA
Printed by Maywood Willis Printing Company. Printed in USA

Also by Dorinda Nicholson

Pearl Harbor Child Video
Dorinda shows a group of students where she lived and describes what happened during the attack and its aftermath. Other survivors tell their stories on-camera, blended with action footage of the attack. Available from our website: www.pearlharborchild.com.

DEDICATION:
Me ke aloha no . . .

Dedicated with deepest aloha to the memory of my mother, **Pansy Ka'ulaleianaikaohukalehua Akona**, and to her nine grandchildren.

Jeff (Makalapa)

Greg (Ka Leo)

Andy (Akona)

Ryan (Ka'ula)

Ishmael III (Ke Alii)

David (Ke Aloha)

Brandon (Ke Koa)

Sean (Ka U'i)

Carmael (Makanaōnalani)

Dorinda Makanaonalani Stagner Nicholson

FOREWORD

Dorinda and I first met on a misty, rainy morning in Hawaii. We were co-presenters, sharing a microphone as we told the story of December 7th for a shipboard audience while circling Ford Island inside Pearl Harbor. Her comments that day were from this book about a native-born child living in the harbor, and were blended with thoughts and perspectives from my military viewpoint and background. Later, our joint presentation, which began in the rain, was ended by an unforgettable double rainbow that appeared as we sailed out of the harbor.

As a WWII submarine commander and later an author of books about war and military history, I have always been fascinated with Pearl Harbor and what happened there. But until I met Dorinda that day, my knowledge of the attack was based on media reports and writings by other military authors and military reports, the reminiscenses of naval persons who were there.

Dorinda's story is different, unique, and remained untold for fifty years, until she wrote this book. At the time of the attack, she was only six years old, but her memories are unforgettable, and Pearl Harbor Child duly chronicles those of her family and some of her friends as well—intense and personal at the same time.

She and her family lived on the Pearl City Peninsula, just across the channel from Ford Island, where lay the moorings of the aircraft carriers and battleships. The old battleship *Utah* was only a few hundred yards from her house. Standing in her front yard, she watched the Japanese torpedo planes scream past at treetop level, strafing her street on their way to attack the American ships anchored peacefully in the harbor. The attacking planes flew so low she could clearly see the goggles on the pilot's faces.

Turning back to look at her house, she saw incendiary bullets skitter across it as parts of the roof caught fire. Not knowing what to do, her father gathered his family into their '39 black Ford, and drove through the smoke-filled streets away from the harbor into the nearby sugarcane fields, where they hid, fearing a Japanese invasion.

She tells us about watching our ships burn in the harbor, and later digging bullets out of her kitchen wall, and what it was like to carry a gas mask everywhere. Dorinda not only provides us with a child's unsophisticated view—from the vantage point of a half a century later, her book also enriches that account with today's deeper understanding.

The original intended audience for this book was children, but to me, the most compelling fact is that it is multigenerational. Today, millions of Americans still have personal family connections to WWII. Pearl Harbor Child will help them strengthen those connections, while giving today's children a first-person account of an event that changed the world.

> Capt. Edward L. Beach US Navy (retired)
> Author of
> > "Run Silent, Run Deep"
> > "Submarine!"
> > "Scapegoats—A Defense of Kimmel and Short at Pearl Harbor"
> > "Around the World Submerged"
> > "The Wreck of the Memphis"
> > "Keepers of the Sea"
> > "Salt and Steel"
> > and many others

Acknowledgments

This book may never have gotten to press without the support of the Arizona Memorial Museum Association. I am indebted to Gary Beito, who brought the concept of *Pearl Harbor Child* to the attention of the Association. It was through his enthusiasm and encouragement and belief that my story needed to be told, that this book became a reality.

My appreciation also goes to those generous individuals who shared their personal photography collections: DeSoto Brown, Abel L. Dolim, and Senator Daniel K. Inouye. Photographs and/or historical props were also provided by the Hawai'i State Archives, Bishop Museum, U.S. Army Museum of Hawai'i, Hawai'i War Records Depository at the University of Hawai'i, with much help from James Cartwright, Johnson County Museum System, National Archives, Harry S. Truman Library, and, of course, the USS *Arizona* Memorial Photo Archives, National Park Service. Also, a note of thanks to Mom and Dad for taking many of the snapshots that found a home inside this book.

Finally, the person most responsible for the completion of this book is my husband, Larry. His creativity shines through in the illustrations, typesetting, editing, and the overall design. He was the one who spent many long and late hours molding my words and weaving illustrations onto the printed page. For his talents, his help, and his love, I am eternally grateful.

D.M.N.

Contents

INTRODUCTION

Years ago, I was told by a member of the Pearl Harbor Survivor's Association that I was too young to remember the attack, and I couldn't have been a civilian survivor of Pearl because, "there were no civilians, much less children, living inside the Harbor." He was wrong. I was there with my family, not on a burning ship, but close enough to see the burning ships anchored near our home.

Today, I still vividly remember watching the attack, I vividly remember the events, and I still remember his doubting comments. At first, I felt discounted and hurt by his skepticism. But now I am grateful. Grateful that it prompted me to ask lots of questions, do some research, and then write *Pearl Harbor Child*.

His doubting comment encouraged me to search for books, memoirs, and articles that might support the fact that civilians did indeed live in Pearl. When I couldn't find any, I began to doubt myself. The evidence that there **was** a neighborhood of civilians on the Pearl City Peninsula unexpectedly surfaced on a map taken from the dead body of a Japanese mini-submarine pilot. His map targeted the position of each ship in the harbor, and also detailed something else: the streets of our small civilian community on the peninsula, including Jean Street, where we lived and where I grew up

December 7, 1941 is "a date that will live in infamy," according to President Roosevelt's famous speech. And for me, and thousands of others, it's true. Each year on that date, my thoughts always turn back to that incredible Sunday when bombs fell on Pearl Harbor. This will be especially true this year, 2001, the 60th anniversary of the attack. As in earlier editions, my story begins with a Hawaiian legend. It shall be no different with this edition, because I want you to know the harbor before the bombs fell.

D.M.N.

Preface: A Pearl Harbor Legend
The Little Yellow Shark *Ka'ehu iki manō o Pu'uloa*

*K*a'ehu was a little yellow shark whose home was in the clear and gentle waters of the Bay of Pu'uloa, known today as Pearl Harbor. The bay was a quiet, peaceful spot in those faraway days when only outrigger canoes were seen, and where the children of Hawai'i played along the shores.

Now, although Ka'ehu's family spoke of him as the little yellow shark, he was not so small. But he was called little because he was young in years. Yes, Ka'ehu was young and also strong, but he was also old with wisdom, for he was a descendant of the shark-god Kamailiili, who had given him wonderful magic powers and had made him very wise.

Ka'ehu had many friends and playmates in the big bay, but sometimes he was filled with longing for his childhood home off the Puna coast on the southern end of the big island of Hawai'i. One day he grew so homesick that he called his shark friends together and told them he was going back to visit his old home. They decided to go with him, and so began the journey from Pearl Harbor along the O'ahu shores to the open sea.

While swimming along outside the reef at Waikīkī, Ka'ehu and his friends met a shark visitor from Maui. His name was Pehu and he was a very different kind of shark from Ka'ehu and his friends.

7

This Maui shark was dangerous, for he was a Man-Eater!

"Why do you swim in just one spot?" asked the little yellow shark although he knew the answer because he was so very wise. He knew that Pehu was eagerly waiting for some unsuspecting surfrider to come out far enough so that he might catch him and have a fine meal for himself.

"I am looking for a crab for my breakfast," Pehu coyly replied. Of course Ka'ehu knew the evil shark was not telling the truth, but he said in a friendly way, "We will help you catch your breakfast. You go and wait and hide yourself alongside the coral reef. My friends and I will go even farther out into the open sea. When the surfriders come, we will drive them toward the shore, and then you can easily catch what you call crab." This greatly pleased the Maui shark, so he went close to the reef and hid himself in its deep shadows.

Then Ka'ehu swam back to his friends and said, "We must destroy this man-eater who will kill our good people. We will all go and push Pehu into the shallow water." Then he and his friends planned how they would save the surfers from the man-eating shark.

There were many surfriders laughing on their surfboards out in the surf, waiting for a rolling wave to ride into shore. Pehu called from his hiding place in the coral reef for the other sharks to come and help him capture his prize. But Ka'ehu called back, "Not yet! Not yet!

We must wait for a better chance!" Ka'ehu had his eyes on two men and the enormously high wave that was bringing them toward shore from out where the high surf begins.

Ka'ehu called, "Now!" as he signalled for his friends to help. Ka'ehu had planned that he and his shark friends would rush in under the enormous wave as it passed over Pehu, and move the men and their surfboards over to one side out of reach of the man-eating shark. And this is just what they did! As Pehu leaped to catch one of the men, the sharks hurled Pehu over the reef and into the shallow water. How they tossed him...over and over, until he plunged deeper and deeper into the sand and could not escape.

The surfriders hurried into shore and breathlessly told everyone what had happened, and that the evil shark who had been destroying some of their people was trapped in the shallow waters. They swam armed with sharp knives to destroy wicked Pehu. When they cut open his body, they found human hair and bones inside the man-eater, proof enough that this was the shark who had been killing some of their people.

The two men who had been surfing and had seen the wonderful feats of the other sharks now understood that the leader of them all was Ka'ehu, the little yellow shark from Pu'uloa or Pearl Harbor, whose ancestors were wise and kind and powerful. Ka'ehu loved the people of O'ahu and hated all evil which could harm them. The men knew then how he had banded together the other good sharks and had used the powers and wisdom given him by the great shark god Kamailiili.

When the body of Pehu was brought ashore, it was cut into pieces and put into baskets. The baskets were carried from Waikīkī to Pelelua, an ancient ceremonial spot, known today as where Nu'uanu and Beretania streets meet in downtown Honolulu.

A large area was cleared to build an immense imu, or oven. The Hawaiian chiefs and village peoples including the kei-ki (Hawaiian name for little children), gathered around the imu and when the fire was an angry red, in went the remains of wicked Pehu. They danced around the fire and chanted old me-le (Hawaiian legends and stories in song), in honor of the occasion where they no longer needed to fear the terrible man-eater. They also chanted their gratitude to Ka'ehu for his good deed. The celebration lasted until the imu fire was nothing but ashes.

All those who saw or heard that the man-eating shark had been captured and killed, knew that it was because of Ka'ehu's cleverness and his love for the people of O'ahu. They never forgot the little yellow shark who lived in the blue waters of Pu'uloa, and how he had saved them!

Author's note:
The hole in the coral reef off Waikīkī where evil Pehu was trapped? It is still known today to many of the old time Hawaiian fishermen.

My Family Moves to Pearl Harbor

1

How I would beg for "Just one more story, please Mom! One more Hawaiian legend, please?" I loved the ones about the fire goddess Pele and her youngest sister Hi'iaka, and especially those about Laka, the hula goddess. Mom was a kumu hula (teacher of Hawaiian dance) and so I often asked her about hula legends and any others that she would tell me.

One day, she told me the legend of the Little Yellow Shark that lived in the Bay of Pu'uloa. She also told me about the shark goddess, Ka'ahupahau, who lived in the same bay full of pearl oysters which is called Pearl Harbor. That's when I first learned that we would be moving to the Pearl City Peninsula, a small strip of land surrounded on three sides by the waters of the Bay of Pu'uloa, better known as Pearl Harbor.

Our house was at 443 Jean Street in the area called Pearl City Peninsula. It was so close to the harbor that Mom could walk to her new job at the Pan American World Airways Clipper Base. She could come home on work days for lunch with my baby brother, Ishmael and our dog, Hula Girl. I was away in kindergarten at Sacred Hearts Convent, and Dad was at work at the Honolulu Post Office. The year was 1940.

Mom, Dad, Ishmael and me in our new front yard on the Pearl City Peninsula.

Passenger service began in 1936, when Pan American Airways flew their famous China Clippers directly into Pearl Harbor. The flight from California took more than 21 hours. The Clippers tied up at a dock just a short distance from our home.

Mom and Dad, all dressed up to greet visitors from the Mainland. Note the water underneath the plane's gangplank.

In those days, children and their parents who came to Hawai'i by airplane flew directly to Pearl Harbor's waters and landed right on the water in a seaplane. The seaplanes, called "China Clippers," looked like flying boats, with four enormous propellers. After the seaplane landed, it would taxi up to a pier just like a motorboat. It would anchor just like a boat, and the passengers would get off onto a rough wooden dock. Mom could clearly see the seaplanes in the harbor from her desk in the library of the Pan American World Airways offices.

To be a child of the harbor was special. My friends and I would take our nets down to the piers where the airplanes were moored, and drop them into the shiny water to catch crabs. The best bait was fish heads, and we tied them to the center of the circular net to lure the crabs. I wanted the best bait, aku heads, so I could attract the most crabs, and especially Samoan crabs, which were the largest of all.

In the fall of 1941, I began first grade at Sacred Hearts Convent in Nu'uanu. But I wouldn't finish out the year there, because of events that were beyond my control, even beyond imagining!

The Japanese carrier Akagi, flagship of Admiral Nagumo, on its way to attack Pearl Harbor. In the foreground, a crewman rests under the wing of a Mitsubishi Zero fighter.

The Zero fighter A1-101 (right background) was the aircraft flown by Lt.Commander Shigeru Itaya, who led the Akagi aircraft to Pearl Harbor. Note the heavy protective covering on the ship's tower.

Meanwhile, somewhere in the Pacific Ocean, the ships of Japanese Admiral Nagumo's Kido Butai (striking force) were making their way eastward through heavy weather and tossing wintry seas toward the Hawaiian Islands.

Three Nakajima torpedo bombers respond to "TORA! TORA! TORA!" the Japanese code words meaning the secret attack was a total surprise to the unsuspecting American fleet.

In that armada, four aircraft carriers would provide a portable airfield for 350 bombers, torpedo planes and Zero fighters. Their deadly mission—to attack the American fleet, peacefully anchored in Pearl Harbor a few hundred yards from my home!

Sunday Morning, December 7, 1941 2

It was Sunday morning and Mom had the radio going. It was a large radio that stood on the floor, with big round knobs that had to be turned to change stations. The music played softly in the living room as Mom began to slice some papaya fruit for breakfast. We could hear the radio from our kitchen table as we sat down to eat our breakfast of Portugese sausage with rice and eggs.

We were not the only ones listening to radio station KGMB's soft music. The station had stayed on the air all night to provide a beacon to help guide a squadron of our B-17 Flying Fortresses as they flew across 2500 miles of ocean from California.

But still another group of planes used the radio broadcast to find their way to the islands. The station unknowingly acted as a guide to two groups of heavily armed planes with red circles on their wings as they flew from the Japanese carriers to execute their surprise attack.

Suddenly we heard the sound of low flying planes, then almost immediately, loud explosions, followed by more planes passing directly over our house. The blasts were too much for my impulsive Scotch-Irish father to ignore. He bolted up from the kitchen table and darted into the front yard. I was right behind him.

ATTACK

We shielded our eyes from the early morning sun and looked up into the orange-red emblem of the Rising Sun. The planes were so low, just barely above the roof tops, that we could see the pilots' faces and even the goggles that covered their eyes.

In the movies, an airplane attack always has the rat-tat-tat of guns as the plane dive-bombs its target. But when these Japanese planes flew directly over us, the sound of the bullets was muffled by the roar of the engines. Even though we couldn't hear them, the incendiary bullets found their targets. Our kitchen was now on fire and parts of the roof were gone. The front door of our next door neighbor was so bullet- ridden from the strafing that it fell from its hinges.

From our end of the peninsula we could see the old battlewagon Utah as it turned on its side in the murky water. Everywhere we looked there was smoke and fire. The odor of burning oil hung over the harbor. All these unbelievable sights and sounds and smells stunned my senses.

I remember the worried expression on my dad's face as he surveyed the chaos around us, and yelled, "Get in the car! We've got to get away from the harbor!"

But as we tried to get into our car, military police in jeeps shouted at everyone to get all civilian cars off the street immediately, driving them up into yards if necessary. We could soon see why, as truckloads of service-men tore by us trying desperately to get to their posts. Many of the men were still dressing, pulling on their pants or shirts or shoes, some even hanging out the tail gate.

The program on the radio was interrupted with dramatic news: "Air raid - Pearl Harbor! This is no maneuver! This is the real McCoy!" This message was later followed by an urgent order for all medical and military personnel to report to the hospitals and bases.

Dad still wanted us to get away, and so Mom, Dad, my baby brother and I piled into our old black Ford, not knowing where we were trying to go, but realizing that we had to find someplace to hide. Dad managed to drive around to another nearby vantage point on the harbor, and what we saw will never be forgotten.

One battleship was upside down and others were ablaze and helpless. We knew that countless men were dying out there. It seemed as if the water was on fire with burning oil. Overhead, we saw a lone Japanese plane calmly make pass after pass through clouds of black smoke rising from the disabled ships. Years later, when photographs of the attack were recovered from Japan, Dad and I looked at the photos and wondered—had they been taken from that plane? We think so.

Battleship Row. Small craft and fireboat assist USS West Virginia in fighting fires. USS Tennessee in the background.

The initial shock of that awful scene was soon replaced with waves of anxiety and panic sweeping over us, and we decided to return home. Dad drove back down the road to the Pearl City Peninsula where we were stopped by military police. In the midst of great confusion and panic, they were in no mood to be cooperative.

Raising their guns, they screamed at us, "Get out of here! You can't go home—it's too dangerous! Find someplace else to stay!"

Not knowing what else to do, Dad turned around and drove our black sedan up Waimano Home Road to the sugarcane fields in the hills above Pearl Harbor.

*Above: Small boat rescues a sailor from the water and two crew members look for ways to escape as fire rages on the USS West Virginia. **Right**: Smoke billows from the USS Arizona. Just ahead of her is the sinking USS West Virginia (far left) and the slightly damaged USS Tennessee.*

WATCHING THE BATTLESHIPS BURN

From the cane fields, we could see the harbor on fire. But most important, we could watch the skies, and if the Japanese planes came back, we could hide ourselves in the tall sugarcane stalks.

But I wasn't thinking about the dive bombers returning. I was thinking about my dog, Hula Girl. She was a black and white mixture, the kind of dog known in Hawai'i as a "poi-dog." I knew she was scared with all of the noisy blasts and explosions, and probably was hiding under my bed. Who was going to feed her and tell her not to be afraid?

Soon our neighbors from Pearl City began to join us in the cane fields. For a little while I forgot about not being able to go home to my dog, because some of my playmates had joined us. As children sometimes do, we forgot about the crisis for awhile. We enjoyed playing, while our parents worried about what to do.

We began to chase each other in and out of the sugarcane stalks laughing and talking. Our only concern was to be careful around the cane, as the leaves sometimes caused itching and you could get small cuts if you weren't careful. For a time, we didn't notice our worried parents, and how they all huddled together talking very seriously while we were busy playing hide and seek.

Our group in the cane field continued to grow. As each car arrived, all the adults rushed up, begging for the latest information. Finally, one of our neighbors joined us with some news.

He said, "I was listening to the radio. Just before noon, Governor Poindexter came on and declared a state of emergency. He said that Hawai'i was to be under martial law, meaning that the military was in charge. Then the Governor ordered all radio stations off the air in case the Japanese came back and tried to use the signals to guide them to the islands for another attack."

We drove our old Ford into the sugarcane fields. It was the only place we could think of to hide.

Our neighbor paused, and then continued. "Then my radio went silent. After that, military police with loudspeakers ordered all civilians on the peninsula to immediately get away from Pearl Harbor, so I came up here."

The Hawaiian sun was now straight up in the sky, and children in the canefields became bored with the games and began to cry. Most of us were hungry. I thought of the unfinished breakfast we left on the kitchen table earlier in the morning. The bananas and papaya would really be o-no (delicious) right now. Maybe my poi-dog Hula Girl had gotten so hungry, that she had gotten the breakfast food. That would be great. But what if she had been hit by a bomb or a bullet? It was then for the first time that I began to cry.

After delivering their bombs, Nakajima Torpedo bombers leave Pearl Harbor and return to the Japanese carriers waiting for them at sea north of Hawaii.

We could still see the smoke from the burning ships in the harbor as we looked down from our hiding place in the mountains. Some of the children slept in the back seat of cars, or on blankets placed on the ground. I sat on the hood of our car with my parents nearby as we continued to watch the harbor burn. I was fine because I was with my parents. With them, I was not afraid.

The grown-ups looked very serious and confused. Unanswered questions flew from their lips. How long were we to stay in the cane fields? What is happening in Honolulu? Have the Japanese forces landed yet? Have they attacked any of the other islands? Will the bombers come back?

If only there was some news to tell us what had happened, and what we were supposed to do! Someone had a shortwave radio, and the adults hovered over it. But there was still no reliable or official information.

We had been attacked, but were we at war? We knew we could not go back to our homes in the harbor. We were refugees. Would we hide in the cane fields and wait for the Japanese attackers to return?

From our vantage point in the cane fields, we kept a watchful eye on the harbor as it continued to burn, sometimes with flames shooting high into the sky as ammunition exploded, followed by another plume of dark, billowy smoke. As the sun dropped closer to the Waianae mountains and we reconciled ourselves to staying in the fields, military police found us. Again, they firmly told us we couldn't go home, and evacuated us to the recreation hall of a sugar mill at Waipahu about ten miles away.

EVACUATION TO A SUGAR MILL

The recreation hall was a small wooden structure that sat on a hill next to the sugar mill. There was a small soup kitchen and one bathroom. Approximately 100 civilian men, women, and children had been brought there. We slept on the floor.

That long night, sitting in total darkness, not knowing whether our homes had been destroyed, or if friends and family were all right, was hard to bear. Telephones were not to be used; they were only for vital military use. Mothers held their children close to them, and people were very gentle and soft-spoken with one another. Always, people took turns trying to get anything on the shortwave radio that would give some news about what was going on.

Then, suddenly, the silence was broken. It sounded as if every available gun on O'ahu had begun firing all at once. We had been told to expect the Japanese back, and this time they would invade. We really thought this was it—the expected invasion!

Red streaks in the night sky came flashing over Pearl Harbor, with sounds of gunfire from all directions. Who was shooting? Had the enemy returned to strike again? What was happening? From Waipahu, we saw the sky light up like an extended lightning storm. Then there was silence. A final question came to us out of the darkness: Had the Japanese landed?

The remainder of the night was spent in fear, wondering what the latest exchange of gunfire meant. The radio was silent, so we had no information. The phones were still restricted to official military use, so we couldn't call anyone to let them know we were safely out of the harbor. There was nothing to do but huddle together in the dark, draw our families close to us, wait for morning, and quietly ponder the unforgettable events of December 7, 1941.

December 8th:
Confusion, Fear and No Information

3

T he smoke from the harbor was clearly visible as my parents strained to see out in the early light. Many hours after the actual attack, we heard occasional sounds of exploding shells, caused when ammunition stored on the battered ships ignited.

Confusion, uncertainty, and fear were on my parents' faces. The radio had been left on all night for any tiny bit of information. The only real news was instructions for all vital personnel to report to work; everyone else was to stay off the streets. Those with medical, military, and government jobs were considered vital. My Dad was a government postal worker at the Honolulu post office near the Iolani Palace. So he reported to work, as did several other fathers from the evacuation center.

Families had little choice when spouses went to work. They simply waited, and hoped for a safe return.

The radio continued to be our lifeline. Everyone in Hawai'i gathered around radios, starved for any information. In the hall, we clustered around a small radio and listened to President Roosevelt broadcast his famous "Day of Infamy" speech that described the attack and asked Congress to declare war against Japan.

Damage was not confined to the military areas of Oahu. Sadly, the damage in Honolulu was the result of our own stray anti-aircraft shells, rather than enemy fire.

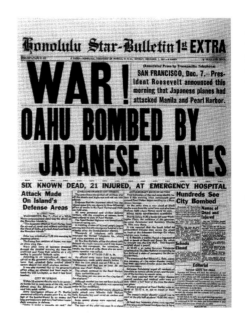

The next few days were spent playing with other children from the Pearl City Peninsula, waiting for parents to return in the evening with news of what was happening. Dad brought a newspaper, but with martial law and the need to keep any useful news from the enemy, the newspaper was heavily censored.

This was a time of rumors and misinformation. No one seemed to have good, reliable information. As a result, people were nervous and upset. Guards were posted everywhere, and if anything suspicious happened, jumpy trigger fingers were ready to fire.

A tragic example of this lack of communication and jumpiness had occurred the night of December 7th. The "Fighting Six," a group of our own fighter planes from the aircraft carrier Enterprise, were trying to land on the island. Sadly, our own overly-nervous troops mistook them for the enemy, and fired at them. This was the cause of the battle sounds and red streaks in the sky we had watched from the evacuation hall. That night, we lost five fighter planes and three pilots from the unfortunate "friendly fire" (see pages 84-85). One of the "Fighting Six" crashed into the Palm Lodge, a small hotel just a block from our home, killing the pilot.

Above Left: Newspapers all over the world screamed news of the attack.
Left: Three civilians were accidentally killed in this car by "friendly fire," some eight miles from Pearl Harbor.

Where's My Dog?

After four or five days of sleeping on the floor at the sugar mill, the Pearl City evacuees were allowed to return home. At last, that meant I could see my dog, Hula Girl again. I couldn't wait.

As we came up our street, I remember peering ahead to see if our house was still there. It was! I was out of the car calling for Hula Girl before Dad even turned off the motor. My parents scurried around to see how much damage had been done, but I went looking everywhere for my dog. Our yard was full of shrapnel and when I couldn't find her, I just knew she had been injured by one of those jagged pieces of metal, and had crawled off somewhere to die.

I searched and called for her for the rest of the day. Dad tried to tell me that she was probably very frightened and was hiding somewhere. He assured me that she would come back very soon. With tears running down my face I kept looking. Up and down the streets I called for her. I even climbed up in the huge mango tree to see if I could see further and yell louder so she could hear me above the house tops. I finally had to come in when it was too dark to keep looking any longer.

Even though it was wonderful to be back in my own bed with sheets and pillows, I could not be consoled. Nothing else mattered to me if I didn't have my dog. She had been my constant companion ever since I could remember.

Mom had me take hula classes when I barely started to toddle, and Hula Girl would come along with us. Then, when Mom began teaching hula in our living room, I'd watch the classes with Hula Girl right at my side. I had given her that name because when she saw me, her happy tail would wag so fast that it made her hips wiggle in her own version of a fast hula dance.

As I lay in my bed, I thought I heard her whimpering under my bed. Quickly, I dropped to the floor and looked under the bed, but it was only my wishful thinking. But soon I heard the whimper again. If it wasn't under my bed - but sounded like it - it could only be from one place. Calling my Dad and grabbing a flashlight, we darted out the front screen door, down the few steps, and looked under the house.

Somehow, when I looked before, I had missed seeing her in that small, dark space. (Homes in Hawai'i don't have basements, and ours was a typical house which sat on short 18-inch stilts leaving just enough room for a crawl space.)

It was a miracle! Hula Girl was there and still alive. She was weak, but strong enough to wag her short tail a couple of twitches. We had a joyous, tearful reunion.

This photo was taken several years later, but still shows the crawl space under our house where Hula Girl hid during the bombing.

Adjusting to a New Life

With Hula Girl at my side, my friends and I spent the next few days playing as if it were summer break time. All schools were closed immediately, and mine was converted into a military hospital. Schools remained closed until February of 1942, almost two months later, so we had many play hours while Hawai'i prepared itself for an expected invasion from Japan.

I watched Mom fill up our bathtub with water, but not to take a bath. She was preparing us in case our water supply was cut off. Some of the rumors said that our water supply might even become poisoned. Mom stayed home with us a lot because her job at Pan American was on hold. The giant sea clipper planes could no longer land in Pearl Harbor. Since the attack, only military aircraft were allowed there.

Many of our play days were spent taking a basket and picking up pieces of shrapnel and seeing who could collect the most. I collected small bullet casings that made a high-pitched whistle sound when you blew on the open end. We also found many bomb casings, and used one for a doorstop for the front door all through the war and afterward.

The bomb casing we picked up in our front yard was used for a doorstop all through the war. One day, we noticed it was missing; someone had stolen it! The Hale Momi sign is for Mom's hula studio. It means "House of Pearl."

In the months following the attack, we often walked down to the tip of the peninsula for a closer look at the battleship *Utah* capsized in the harbor. It is still there today, just around Ford Island from the USS *Arizona*. The *Utah* has 58 men entombed in her hull, while the *Arizona* lost 1,177 men, most of them still aboard their ship.

Today, both are memorials to the men who died there. The USS *Arizona* allows visitors to come on board its memorial, and nearly 2 million do so each year to pay their respect.

The USS Utah capsized just off Ford Island. The USS Raleigh is in the distance.

The USS Arizona, as it looked after the fires were out, resting in 40 feet of water. Years later, the Memorial was built directly over her submerged hull.

Dad kept finding bullets in the walls of our house, especially the kitchen. These were incendiary bullets that were supposed to burn when hitting a target. Parts of our kitchen did catch on fire, and the blackened streaks were how we could tell the path of the bullets and where they had stopped. I still have a bullet that dad cut out of the wall above the phone with his pocket knife.

Dad spent long hours at the post office. One of his jobs was working with the mail that was salvaged from the *Arizona* and *Oklahoma* battleships. The salvaged mail was brought by the Navy to two big rooms in the Federal building, where about a dozen people sorted it. Not only was this mail wet, some of it was also burned. Dad and the other postal workers searched the damaged mail for names and addresses, trying to find enough information to send those letters where they were supposed to go.

Above: This bullet was lodged in the wall of our kitchen. Mom carried it in her coin purse for the rest of her life. It is the only one I still have of the many that struck our house.
Left: At the time of the attack, Pearl City was a rural area, and had its own railroad train which made frequent runs back and forth into the city. For several years, my brother and I rode from this station to school in Honolulu, and thought it was fun.

FOOD BECOMES SCARCE

We had two grocery stores in our area. If there was any panic after the bombing, it was over food. Everyone was concerned, because the ships that brought food from the mainland might not be able to come, and supplies could be cut off completely. Lines formed at grocery stores and people tried to buy everything. To avoid a mob, only a few people would be let in the store at a time, and then sometimes only if the storeowners knew you and your family. This was a "special" kind of rationing that began even before the official ration stamps were printed and in use.

Next, the military governor immediately urged all non-essential civilians to leave. This meant everyone who did not have a job crucial to the war effort. The reason? Fewer mouths to feed, and fewer people to defend when the enemy returned. The wives and children of the military were forced to leave. Residents could stay or go. Some of my friends at school were sent to the mainland to live with family until the war was over. But the islands were home to my Hawaiian mother, and she couldn't bear to leave. We chose to stay.

Since much of Hawai'i's food must be imported, people were very worried. Long lines became an overnight fact of life, even for barefoot kids and poi-dogs.

Immediately after Pearl Harbor, the steamship lines were swamped with people who wanted to leave Hawai'i and return to the mainland.

Hawai'i in the War Years

6

All of Hawai'i prepared for the time when the Japanese would return and attempt to occupy the islands with their troops. There weren't enough soldiers to do everything in the frantic rush to protect the islands, so everyone—children, moms, dads— thousands of civilians all pitched in to help. One of the first requirements from the military rule was that everyone over six years old had to be fingerprinted and carry an I.D. card at all times. Schoolteachers helped by going door to door, since school was called off for weeks while the islands geared up for war. My Mom and Dad never did tell me that not only was the identification card to keep out enemy saboteurs, but it was to identify the body in case of bombing raids.

UGLY BARBED WIRE AND DINGY BOMB SHELTERS

One of the first tasks was to clear land and put up barbed wire all around the island coast line. Even our famous Waikīkī beach had rolls and rolls of ugly barbed wire stretched across the sand leading to the ocean.

For protection against bombs and flying bullets, bomb shelters and

The effects of the war were seen everywhere, including barb wire on Waikīkī Beach.

A new bomb shelter, clean and dry. They didn't stay that way very long.

trenches were constructed. These were especially important at schools. Our school had a bomb shelter, but most of us were scared to go inside because it was dark, smelled bad, and had bugs. One day at school, the air raid warnings sounded and we grabbed our gas masks and went dutifully to the air raid shelter. When we got there, it had filled with water from a rain the night before. We all cheered when we didn't have to go inside.

The military government demanded that each house build its own shelter. I remember my dad trying to dig a shelter for us in our back yard. He got his shovel and started scooping out the dirt. Living in the middle of a harbor, our dirt was mostly sandy and marsh-like. So dad only dug about ten shovels full before the hole filled up with water. We never did have our very own bomb shelter and I was glad. There was no way I was going down into those dark, damp holes, bullets or not.

CAMOUFLAGE AND BAYONETS

I did like the lacy camouflage netting, however. We had a lot of it on the Pearl City Peninsula to cover up some of the military installations that had large artillery guns. The netting went over the tops of the huge guns and kept them hidden from the air. The fabric was dyed brown and green, and woven into a net which looked like trees, grass and dirt.

Seen from below, strips of fabric, attached to netting, helped conceal military objects and materials.

Even some buildings in downtown Honolulu were painted green and brown. But camouflage paint on the buildings didn't work as well. They still looked like buildings, but with funny colors on them. Sand bags were placed in front of several, with soldiers standing guard with rifles and bayonets.

The bayonets always terrified me. I never even looked at the soldiers' faces. All I could see was the sharp point of the knife on the end of the long gun. I knew that these were American soldiers, on my side, and there to protect me, but it didn't matter.

Above: Sandbags and bayonets in downtown Honolulu.
Right: Structures like the Aloha Tower were too large to be hidden under camouflage nets, so they were painted with irregular patterns in an attempt to make them less visible from the air. During the war, women joined the armed forces in record numbers.

When my school became a military hospital, I went to a school in downtown Honolulu next to the Governor's home. At the entrance to the governor's home were two soldiers with the largest bayonets I had ever seen. These were the two that I feared the most. Every day before and after school, I would cross the street and walk a block out of my way just to avoid looking or even coming close to those guns armed with their long, sharp knife blades.

GAS MASKS

Hawai'i was worried about the use of poison gas by Japan, and so every person in the islands was issued a gas mask. They were to be carried everywhere at all times.

Even the telephone operators were issued gas masks, but I don't know how often they wore them. I suspect this operator just put hers on for the picture.

Mine felt heavy across my left shoulder in its brown canvas bag. My brother was only two, and his mask was almost as long as he was. Even babies had to have them. The infant version was really comical. It was actually a bag to slip into, with big bunny ears on top for decoration and a see-through window to look out of. Most of the mothers complained that their babies were afraid to be put into them. Mom said it made her very sad to watch me trudge off to school carrying my gas mask.

To be sure that everyone knew what to do in case of an attack, and to give emergency crews a chance to practice, regular drills were conducted. My Mom and Dad were air raid wardens and guided the drills with make-believe bomb bursts. My favorite part was to be a make-believe "casualty," stretched out on the side of the road waiting for a volunteer ambulance crew to find me and bandage my "injuries."

MONEY

Hawai'i was always preparing for the Japanese to return. If that occurred, the enemy would quickly seize the banks and use the American money to buy weapons or goods in other countries. To protect against that possibility, Mom and Dad, and all other Hawai'i residents, had to take their money and turn it into the bank. The bank replaced it with special currency that had "Hawaii" overprinted on both sides. This was the only legal tender for the islands during most of the war.

*Above: My brother Ish and I, obeying the wartime rules to always carry our gas masks. **Below**: During the war, all paper money had "Hawaii" printed on it.*

BLACKOUTS AND CURFEWS

Even the blackouts were fun—at first. We could have no lights on after dark, and it was fun to figure out how to eat in the dark when you couldn't see your food or anyone at the table. How we would rush to get everything done before dark! At first, it meant taking my flashlight into the closet and looking at picture books or listening to the radio while in there. That was an adventure, until it also meant there was nothing else to do but go to bed when it got dark. That's when I decided it wasn't fun anymore.

Before long, Mom and Dad, like all our neighbors, bought some black enamel paint and painted our windows black. Some people used black tar paper to cover their windows. Then we could turn our lights on, but with the windows and doors closed up, it became very stuffy. We weren't among the lucky ones who had an electric fan before the war, and it was impossible to get one after the war started. Boy, was it sticky and hot!

We had to be extremely careful about any light escaping from our house, because the block warden was very strict. If he saw any light, he would report it to soldiers in a patrol car. They took care of the problem by simply shooting out the light!

One time, Mom was rushing to get the wash done on the back porch with the aid of a flashlight. She was there just long enough to put a load into our old-fashioned wringer washing machine. But she wasn't quick enough, and the warden appeared, demanded that she turn off the flashlight, and threatened to take her immediately to military court. Several of our neighbors had been taken to court, sentenced and fined for just a slight, faint glow of light. Mom never washed another load of laundry after dark during the war.

Can you imagine how dark it would be with no street lights, no lighted signs on buildings, no lights in homes and no car lights? That's right, no car lights either. In addition to blackouts, there were strict curfews. No one could be on the streets after dark without a special pass. If you had a pass, you could be out after dark, but your car lights had to have a hood over them to cover most of the light.

Headlights of our '39 Ford Sedan had to be covered with a shield to force all the light downward. While Dad was photographing the car, he wanted me to get into the act.

My Dad had a pass to be on the street after dark because his job at the Post Office required him to work long hours. Our Ford sedan's headlights had a shield over them that looked to me like the eyes of a sleepy cat with eyelashes.

Dad was stopped many times when out at night, sometimes by military police, and sometimes by a volunteer civil defense guard. One night when he tried to drive home, he was stopped three times and had to show his permit and identification card while the flashlight was aimed first at his face and then at the card, making sure he was the person on the permit.

Each car had its own headlight shield design. None of them were very attractive.

A couple, who were among Mom and Dad's best friends, often came to visit us for Sunday dinner. We had to plan carefully for them to come early enough to get home before dark, or arrange for them to spend the night in our little two-bedroom house. One time, they didn't leave soon enough and it got dark before they could get home. They had to spend the night in their car, and finish their drive home when the sun came up the next morning.

CENSORSHIP

Censorship was a fact of life during the war years, and because of the critical importance of Pearl Harbor to our armed forces, all types of communications were censored, including newspapers, magazines, radio broadcasts, and even the U.S. Mail. Part of my Dad's job during the early part of the war was to censor the civilian mail.

On the second floor of the Honolulu post office, hundreds of readers would censor the civilian mail, and ink out or cut out any parts that were judged to be unacceptable or hurtful to the war effort. The Army and Navy had censors of their own. The objective for both civilian and military censors was to prevent any important military-related facts from falling into Japanese hands.

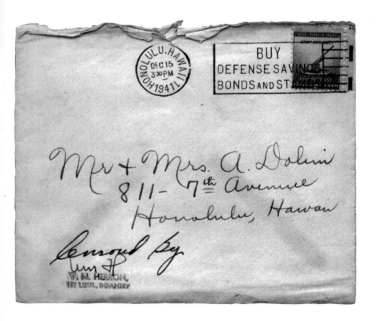

This letter was received by the Dolim family only a few days after the Pearl Harbor attack. Note that censorship was already in effect.

Strangely, one forbidden topic was the weather. If you mentioned the weather, it would be cut out of your letter. Even the newspapers could not mention forecasts or current weather, since this might help the enemy plan an attack.

Dad said that sometimes when a letter left the post office after the censors had finished with it, there were so many pieces cut out—that it looked like pieces of confetti in the envelope!

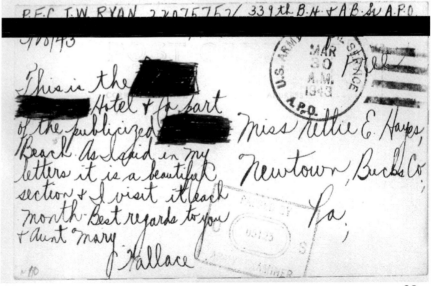

*Above: This postcard, sent from Hawaii to New Jersey, shows the "passed" stamp applied by the censor. **Below:** On this card, the censor crudely marked through the names of the hotel and beach.*

RATIONING

Across America, there were many shortages during the war. But in Hawai'i, we had shortages of **everything**! Rationing was the system used to deal with the problem. Rationing was a way to provide everyone with a fair share of things that were scarce. It was supposed to keep prices low, and make sure that people got what they needed. Since most products and supplies came to our islands by boat through possible enemy waters, the military had first priority on all goods.

One of the main shortages was gasoline. At first, gas rationing required coupons that were good for five gallons apiece, with a limit of two per month. The coupons were based on an A-B-C system with "A" being the lowest amount. Dad got a higher allotment because his post office job was considered vital, and he had to drive to work from Pearl City Peninsula to downtown Honolulu. There was a lettered sticker attached to his front windshield that dictated how much gas he could have. He had to turn in the required amount of coupons, which allowed him to purchase the gasoline. He and Mom spent many hours trying to carefully budget their use of coupons and the tiny ration stamps for the necessities of life.

Since coupons like these were needed to purchase gasoline, people could only buy a few gallons at a time, so they planned their driving very carefully.

Eggs were too expensive to buy, and even if you could find meat in the stores, it was also too expensive. That was when I first learned to like peanut butter, and beans, both foods that Dad introduced to our family. When we could get peanut butter, Dad would mix the oil off the top into the peanut mixture. At first I thought it was awful, like the beans he used to cook on the back of the kerosene stove. We ate a lot of beans with onions, and even a scrap of ham if we could get some.

Butter was scarce also. But we could sometimes get margarine. It came in a white sack with an orange-colored tablet. It was my job to take the white oleomargarine, put it in a bowl and mix in the orange tablet until it all became yellow. Later in the war, the tablet was replaced by a liquid in a plastic pouch, which made it easier to color the margarine to look like butter. Many Friday nights were spent around the kitchen table, kneading and mixing the white stuff into butter-looking stuff.

Many times, there was no toilet paper at the grocery stores. Just as the metal can of maple syrup shaped like a log cabin disappeared from the shelves, toilet paper was another of many things the stores couldn't keep in stock. Mom would save paper, usually newspaper, and rub it back and forth against itself to soften it, and that became our toilet paper. There was no way you could call it toilet tissue.

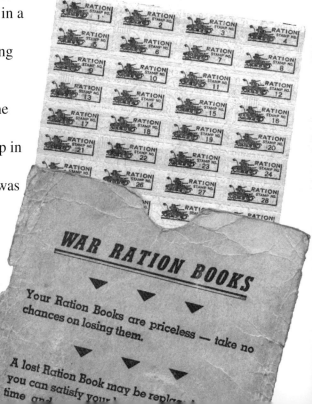

Across America, children and their families had to deal with shortages, and ration books became a way of life.

Mom and her lady friends couldn't get hosiery to wear on their legs for dress-up occasions. They were called silk stockings then. Her friends would put makeup on their legs to make them look like they were wearing silk stockings. Then they would draw a seam line up the back of their legs, because all hose then had seams. But Mom's legs were naturally brown, so she didn't have to paint her legs.

We all had to get used to doing with less of what was considered non-essential. But, like most kids, I missed candy and stuff with sugar, and you know what I missed the most? It was gum! Especially bubble gum.

Seamed stockings like these were very fashionable in the 1940's. The only problem was, you couldn't get them during the war, because nylon was needed for military uses such as parachutes.

Salvage, Victory Gardens and War Bonds

7

Our armed forces needed huge amounts of metal and rubber for planes, tanks, and ships. It was difficult to get rubber because the Japanese were patrolling the Pacific Ocean, cutting America off from rubber supplies in Asia. So, everyone was asked to gather and turn in any kind of rubber as a contribution to the war effort.

Hawaii's children, as well as mainland children, went door to door collecting what we could for rubber salvage. We gathered old tires, along with shoe heels, toys, sink stoppers, and even old bathing caps.

These Hawai'i Scouts are doing their part by collecting old tires to be recycled for use on combat vehicles.

43

Above: *When America went to war, women workers were needed everywhere to help in the defense effort. No longer doing "women's work," many became experts at building tanks, ships, and airplanes.* *Right:* *Children all over the USA collected scrap metal, including everything from old appliances to tin cans to pots and pans, as did these students at Kapalama School.*

Metal salvage included appliances, tin cans, pots and pans, anything that contained some metal. We even saved every bit of tin foil from gum wrappers when we were lucky enough to get some gum. We took each piece of foil and rolled it into a ball. As we added each new piece, we had a larger and larger ball to donate for the war. One friend said she knew that her ball of tin foil was going to be made into the bullet that would win the war.

VICTORY GARDENS

With the warm weather of the islands, and scarce supplies that must come by boat, Hawai'i was already well on its way to Victory Gardens before the mainland joined in. Children worked in the gardens alongside the whole family, planting vegetables. There were large community gardens in parks, vacant lots, churches, anywhere there was an unused plot of ground. People with a small amount of land just piled dirt on top of their air raid shelters to make room to grow their food.

We had enough room in our back yard to grow many different kinds of vegetables. My job was to hoe the weeds, and I hated it.   I complained, and when that didn't work, I pouted. When I pouted, I wasn't allowed to go to the Saturday afternoon movie, which was our major form of entertainment in those days.

Because we also had a meat shortage, my dad said we were going to grow another crop that he called, "Pearl City Chicken." Calling it that was just to fool me, because he knew that I would eat chickens, but not what he really had planned. Without saying much, Dad built wooden cages above the ground, called hutches. After that, he bought some rabbits, and I eventually learned that they were to be a new food source for the family. But not for me!

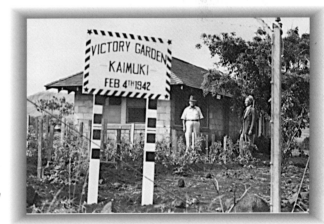

Civilians who didn't have garden space combined their efforts in community gardens like this one.

The rabbits were an Angora breed with lots of fluffy fur. I named the first one, "Patches," and called his mate, "Mrs. Patches." I also named all of their babies. Loudly I would plead with daddy, begging him not to kill the rabbits for food. You can probably guess what happened next.

To save the rabbits, I began to hoe the garden, and pull the weeds without complaining. And I even learned to like vegetables.

WAR BONDS AND STAMPS

The war effort needed great sums of money to pay for the increasing cost of the war. War bonds were used to raise money for the guns, bombs and bullets. A war bond was a special savings account. In effect, the people were loaning money to our country, to be paid back later with interest. Hawaiians were unusually patriotic, and in every sale of war bonds, we exceeded the goal set by the government .

War bonds were sold everywhere—in stores, post offices, door to door, and even along the sidewalks. If you somehow managed to avoid buying one, you would likely receive one for your birthday or Christmas.

The way Hawaii's children helped with bonds was by buying individual saving stamps, which went into a special book. I bought 25 cent stamps to lick and stick in my stamp book. I would go without lunch to buy the stamps, until I had filled my book with $18.75 in stamps, ready to take to the post office to trade for my war bond. By buying a few stamps at a time, even children like myself could help.

Even school kids could help raise money for the war effort, by buying one stamp at a time.

The War Drags On

8

With each passing year, more and more military personnel came to the islands. They were either on their way to battle, or returning, injured, to recuperate in Hawaii's hospitals. Eventually, the armed forces population on my island of O'ahu outnumbered the civilian population. There were men (many of them still looked like boys) in uniform everywhere.

My Mom, like other island mothers, was afraid for her daughter to be around so many men. I was not allowed to be anywhere near the section of Honolulu called the "Hotel Street" area. I couldn't even ride a bus through that part of the city because she didn't want me to see all the bars, tattoo shops, and honky-tonk photo shops.

The Hotel Street area was a major attraction for off-duty servicemen.

We Can Do It!

Mom had always been a working mother, with a job away from home. This was unusual for the 1940's, when most moms stayed at home with their children. But after Pearl Harbor, when the men went to war, the women went to work, and the government encouraged them to do so. It was common for women to work at jobs that previously only men had held. So Mom joined other working mothers, and also worked many hours overtime daily. Then she came home and taught her hula classes, and still tried to take care of my brother and me. It was difficult, but that's the way most families lived during the war years.

Other evidence that we were at war came from posters that were seen everywhere. They warned us about enemy spies, and urged us to support the war effort. There was no escape from the reality of wartime at movie theaters either. The newsreels were always about the war. Often, the cartoon characters were in the Army or Navy, and were doing their part against the enemy. Even the main feature would often have a war theme, as well as the comedies, which were supposed to make us laugh.

GIVE IT YOUR BEST!

War Posters-Left above: Symbol of the importance of women in the war effort. Left below: A stern Uncle Sam promoted security. Left: A 48-star American flag urged us to work even harder.

48

Morale could be a problem. Everyone needed to be cheered up occasionally. The movies were a good way to do that, and on some Saturday nights there would be live entertainment after the main feature. Mom's hula students, known as the Hale Momi girls, which included me as the littlest dancer, entertained at some of the programs. I loved to dance, especially when wearing my favorite hula costume, a holoku. This is a long fitted dress, that flows out into a train like a wedding dress. Fresh flower leis matched the colors in our holoku. I also loved to wear a flower in my hair, even though it kept sliding off. I especially liked the holoku ever since my hula skirt fell off when I was trying to dance in Mom's show at the Lalani Hawaiian Village in Waikiki when I was barely three.

Local entertainers couldn't handle all the demand for shows, and so the U.S.O. came to the islands. One even came to my school. They sang songs like, "Praise the Lord and Pass the Ammunition." I remember trying to figure out how the U.S.O. showgirls got their eyelids to be blue. I had never seen blue eyelids before, and I thought they were so glamorous.

| Jimmy Wilbert | Dorinda (me) | KaNani Austen | Lydia Hironaka | LaVerne Blackburn | Pansy (Mom) |

Part of the Hale Momi dance troupe, all dressed up to present "Pearl City Frolic" at the Princess Theater. Mom's troupe, like others, entertained often during the war.

The United Service Organization (USO), mostly volunteers, provided recreation facilities for American troops and gave them "a home away from home."

Some of my friends were jealous that U.S.O. shows didn't come to their schools because they had school in private homes, usually on the front porch. But their jealousy was a small matter. Another problem was far more serious.

You see, these friends were of Japanese ancestry. Their small, one-story wood house had a special banner in the window. The banner displayed a gold star for their son, who was killed while serving the Army in Europe. This young man had joined the U.S. Army and served with the colorful 442nd Regiment from Hawai'i, which is a story in itself.

A "Star in the Window" was a symbol of great respect, indicating that someone who lived in this house was either in military service or had died in service for his or her country.

Japanese-Americans in Hawai'i

9

Many people don't know what happened to the Japanese-Americans who were already living in Hawai'i at the time of the Pearl Harbor attack. Within a week after December 7th, about 300 of them were sent to a detention camp on Sand Island, not far from the Honolulu airport. Eventually, over 1,400 local Japanese were isolated there. Many were sent to the mainland, to be held there against their will.

Sand Island, in the Honolulu harbor, is where many Japanese-Americans (along with a small number of European-born suspects) were forced to move after the Pearl Harbor attack. A small "city" of tents and cots was quickly built to house them.

Fortunately, the bulk of the Japanese-American citizens of Hawai'i escaped being sent to these prison camps, because it was impossible to isolate about 150,000 people living on several islands. There simply wasn't room to do that. Unfortunately, the Japanese-Americans living on the mainland, numbering more than 120,000, were not so lucky. They didn't have thousands of miles of Pacific Ocean to keep them from a prison camp, and many of them lost everything they owned.

Finally, after more than 50 years, some Japanese-Americans have received an official apology from the U.S. Government, and money to help make up for the treatment they received. Sadly, many have died through the years without knowing that one day the great error would be recognized. Some of their children took the letter of apology to the graves of their parents to show that at last, the government had admitted its mistake.

Senator Daniel Inouye, a former member of the 442nd Regiment from Hawai'i, was pleased with the final outcome.

"When Congress passed the Reparations Bill, this was a proud day for America. It takes a big country to admit wrong. Many countries would not do this."

Daniel K. Inouye
U.S. Senator from Hawai'i

Even though many of the island Japanese weren't imprisoned, they still faced a difficult and frightening time. Suspicion and outright hatred were sometimes directed at them. A few changed their last names. Many of them Americanized their first names. For example, my friend Eiko changed her name to Eileen.

Many of the island Japanese wanted to prove their loyalty to America, the country they had accepted as their own. Even though they had been born in Hawai'i and were U.S. citizens, there was much concern over

Above: Senator Daniel K. Inouye is a former member of the 442nd Combat Group, whose slogan, "Go For Broke" is island pidgin (slang) which means something like, "you can do it." Below: Inouye in his Army uniform on patrol in the mountains of Italy, where the "fighting 442nd" made a distinguished contribution to our war effort in Europe.

where their true loyalties lay. At first, when Japanese-Americans wanted to enlist in the armed services, they were not accepted. To prove their loyalty, some became volunteers who did hard manual labor for the Army. But it wasn't until January, 1943, before any were accepted. They quickly made up for lost time.

General Mark Clark reviews the 442nd. The extraordinary toughness, discipline and motivation of this unit made believers out of those who had doubted their loyalty and ability.

THE FIGHTING 442ND REGIMENT

Over 9,500 AJA's (Americans of Japanese Ancestry) volunteered for the Army, and about 2,700 were accepted. To avoid the confusion of Japanese-Americans fighting against Japan, these new volunteers were trained to fight against America's other major enemy in World War II, the Nazi's. Thousands of people turned out to cheer the new recruits when they sailed from the islands to fight in Europe. They served as the 442nd Regiment, and by the end of the war were honored as the most decorated unit in the entire American army.

The men of the Fighting 442nd had proven their loyalty!

Other Japanese-Americans did also. In fact, as early as January, 1942, a Honolulu newspaper stated that no espionage could be traced to the local population. Later, an FBI agent was quoted as saying he found the vast majority of the island Japanese to be loyal, honest, and hard-working citizens.

Above: The Famed 100th Battalion of the 442nd Regiment passes the reviewing stand at Kapi'olani Park. **Left:** *The Regiment, some wearing leis, stands at parade rest on the grounds of the Iolani Palace.*

War is Over—Peace At Last!

10

Through the long war years, Mom continued to teach her hula classes at our home, and graduated many students at her yearly u-ni-ki (recital). By now, her hula classes also included wives and women stationed with the military at Pearl Harbor. In 1945, our military forces finally decided to end the blackouts and curfews, so each weekday evening she taught her students, very precisely, the graceful art of hula.

Mom thought we should cancel hula class the day of August 14, 1945. The news had just come that Japan had agreed to surrender, and she thought that her teenage students wouldn't want to come to lessons. But she was wrong. They wanted to come and be together that night. We had class, and then it was time for Mom to drive one of her students home. As we began our drive back through Pearl City, just as our car passed the courthouse, crowds of our friends and some neighbors surrounded all the cars on the road.

Suddenly, firecrackers exploded all around us. At first, it scared me, thinking that our car would catch on fire. But we were safe. People were just letting off steam. Mom sounded her horn, and we inched our way through the ecstatic celebration. Our neighbors paraded through the streets, banging pots and pans together and chanting, "The war is over." We drove farther down the peninsula until we could see the fireworks from the harbor, and hear the air raid sirens wailing along with the gas alarm gongs and whistles from the ships.

The sky over the harbor was flashing brightly with flares, each one adding its note in a symphony of light. The air was filled with all variety of ship's whistles adding their voices to the sirens and gongs in an unforgettable scene. In a spontaneous eruption of joy and excitement, people hugged and kissed anyone close to them.

Our old black Ford inched through the crowds, and slowly came down Lehua Avenue, making a right turn into our street. As we came closer to the house, our car lights picked up the white uniform of a sailor standing in a yard across the street. Unlike the others, he was alone. I watched him curiously, wondering why he wasn't with the jubilant crowds nearby. Then I saw that he had his own way to express his joy at America's victory. He leaned against a palm tree with his elbow bent, and rested his face in the crook of his arm. I didn't hear him cry, but I could see his shoulders and head quake with emotion.

The war was over.

Above: Staff Sgt. Michael S. Padeken of the 442nd Combat Team is joyously welcomed home by his family. Below: American servicemen celebrate VJ-Day in downtown Honolulu.

Surrender Document Signed on Battleship USS *Missouri*

11

By the end of the war, I had become used to having spent most of my childhood surrounded by the sights and sounds, the comings and goings of troops, and the headlines of war.

One of those headlines caused great confusion and concern in my family and many others. It told about something called the atomic bomb, and how it had been exploded in Japan and had wiped out a city, killing many people. We wondered how a single bomb could do so much damage. Radio newscasts also told the gruesome details of the enormous devastation that resulted. And then President Harry S. Truman made a radio broadcast to explain the American action.

He said, "I realize the tragic significance of the atomic bomb . . . Having found the bomb we have used it. We have used it against those who attacked us without warning at Pearl Harbor . . . We shall continue to use it until we completely destroy Japan's power to make war. Only a Japanese surrender will stop us."

Shortly thereafter came the Japanese surrender. When President Truman gave the announcement, the release from the tension of all the war years was electrifying, and our concern over the terrible bomb was put aside as the entire world sighed with relief at the prospect of peace.

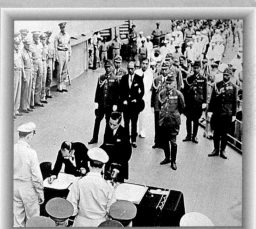

The USS Missouri was the site for the signing of the surrender document ending WWII

The high emotions were replaced by a feeling of solemnity for the signing that ended World War II, on September 2, 1945, shortly after 9:00 a.m. The formal ceremony took place in Tokyo Bay, aboard the battleship USS *Missouri*, as our B-29 bombers circled watchfully overhead. General Douglas MacArthur presided over the ceremony on the great ship's deck, flanked by Admirals Halsey and Nimitz, plus many others. Foreign Minister Shigemitsu and General Umezu signed for the Japanese delegation. Admiral Nimitz signed for the United States, and General MacArthur signed as the Supreme Allied Commander.

The years of war were ended by a few marks on paper!

When MacArthur accepted the surrender documents, he said, "Let us pray that peace be now restored to the world, and that God will preserve it always. These proceedings are now closed."

Above: Admiral Nimitz signs the Surrender documents as MacArthur, Halsey and many others observe. Left: The signature page of the Instrument of Surrender.

With the USS Arizona close by, former enemies Richard Fiske and Zenji Abe participate in the historic "Friendship Meeting" on board the USS Missouri (see page 72).

Times have changed since that day on the USS *Missouri*. No one could have forseen how the former enemies, Japan and America, would evolve into allies and friends. This is truly an amazing turn of events.

But warm feelings are still not unanimous. There are some Americans whose hatred is so deep, and whose loss of family or friends was so great, that they are still unable to forgive and forget.

Still, there are others who say, "It's been 60 years now. When you stop and think about it, the Japanese soldiers were doing their jobs, and we were doing ours. It just happened that our jobs were to kill each other."

For those who were willing to face the difficulty of healing old wounds, a special ceremony was held on December 6, 2000, at a special place—on the very same deck where the WWII treaty was signed!

A group of Japanese veterans, three of whom actually participated in the Pearl Harbor attack, returned to the harbor for this ceremony. One of them was Zenji Abe, who flew a torpedo bomber on December 7, 1941, and who has become great friends with our friend, Richard Fiske, the bugler from the USS *West Virginia*. Both men were asked to speak to those assembled and describe how they felt about what was happening. It was a very emotional experience for everyone.

There were speeches in English and Japanese, with translation into both languages. Finally, a row of American veterans stood facing a row of their former enemies. It was a special moment, and I held my breath, wondering if anything would disturb this unique occasion.

But thankfully, nothing happened. No one moved until the two facing rows shook hands and exchanged Hawaiian leis in a symbol of friendship. Then, all those present were invited to place their signatures on two large banners, one to be sent to Japan, and the other to remain in Hawaii. Larry, my husband, and I also signed the banners, grateful to be witnesses to this historic moment.

Upper Left: *A former Japanese pilot meets Daniel Martinez of the National Park Service and several American WWII veterans.* *Upper Right:* *Richard Fiske (center) and others sign the commemorative banners.* *Lower Left:* *Standing at the exact spot where the peace treaty was signed in 1945, enthusiastic handshakes are exchanged in a concluding ceremony.*

60

The Navy Takes Our Home

12

The surrender treaty was signed in September, and in October, I celebrated my 10th birthday. Mom and dad surprised me with a new dress that came all the way from the mainland. The dress had beautiful embroidery on the skirt, and even a matching blue "beanie" hat with red trim. On that birthday in peacetime Hawaii, our family thought we could always live in Pearl Harbor, but it was not to be.

We tried very hard to keep our home, but now that the fighting was over, the Navy could concentrate on moving the civilian locals out of the harbor. My dad formed the Pearl City Peninsula Association, to join with our neighbors to see if we could keep from losing our land. The association wrote letters to the newspapers about the United States Navy intimidating ordinary working people who were natives of the islands, and stealing our homes.

We put up a long, hard fight, but all civilian property was condemned on the peninsula. We had to sign our deed over to the Navy, and then were required to pay rent. By this time, most of our neighbors gave up and left. Some took their houses with them. One of my last memories of Jean Street was our Filipino neighbor's house, cut in two like a deli sandwich, being towed down our street away from the harbor.

Finally, it was time to leave. I didn't want to go. The only life I had known had been that of a child of the harbor, of crab nets, fishing off the pier, Pan-American China Clippers, and a world war.

A present for my 10th birthday—a new dress!

A few other civilians had hurriedly left as soon after December 7th as they could. But our family never wanted to leave, and we were among the last civilians to do so, staying in our house in Pearl City until my junior year of high school. We had doggedly held out for more than 7 years after the war ended.

Still feeling the emotional ties to the harbor, we knew we could never completely leave it. So, we built our new home up in the hills of Halawa Heights, where we could see the harbor from every room, although now it was from quite a distance. It was close enough, however, that if I looked just forward of Ford Island, I could barely see the movement of the American flag that still flew proudly from the temporary platform over the sunken remains of the battleship USS *Arizona*.

This gate leads to a beautiful home on the peninsula, now used for officer housing. This is the only exceptional house that remains.

This view from our house in Halawa Heights shows a carrier docked at Ford Island.

A Sad Farewell to the Harbor

13

T hen, as now, I still say goodbye so regretfully, feeling that my soul is a part of the harbor and peninsula. I can't explain the feeling, except that my old home is so full of emotions and memories for me. Each time I return, the harbor and pier beckon me to the water's edge. I look for the Pan American Clipper marker, detailing the landing of the first Clipper plane from the mainland.

Right: Years ago, I took my two oldest sons, Jeff and Greg, to show them where I played on this pier when I was "a child of the harbor."
Above: *Not far away is the marker showing where the China Clippers used to land.*

A two-man Japanese midget submarine like this one silently slid into Pearl Harbor on December 7th. Ironically, it was sunk by the USS Ward near my old pier, about an hour before the first bombs fell.

Close by is another marker noting that a midget Japanese submarine had also shared this part of the harbor, but on a secret, deadly mission on a fateful December morning many years ago.

When I look at my old pier, it pains me to see that it has aged even more, and now it has been barricaded because of wood rot. But I still see it through the eyes of a child as the place where I spent many hours with my crab nets. This is where I rode my bicycle as faithful Hula Girl ran along beside me.

Just down the pier along the coastline is where the cracked foundation still sits empty of the old Pan American clipper base. A banyan tree now grows where the old Palms Hotel burned in the fiery crash of the American fighter plane off the USS *Enterprise* (our own guns mistakenly shot him down the evening of December 7, 1941). Across the channel, I search for a glimpse of the rusting hull of the USS *Utah*, laying on its side. It's difficult to see her now that navy housing fills the horizon. Each part of my journey along the harbor shoreline floods me with memories, not only of the day the bombs fell, but of a farewell to a childhood lost in a world war.

At the National Memorial Cemetery of the Pacific - Punchbowl, a flower lei honors the memory of those whose story will never be told.

The final farewell to the harbor finds me at the silent gray marble wall in the USS *Arizona* Memorial.
As a child of the harbor, the memory of the day the bombs fell will remain with me always.

Epilogue—Discovering Our Pearl Harbor Bond

Richard
Fiske

Jim Daniels

Thompson Izawa

Hazel and Tetsu Kobashigawa

Melvin
(Jonesie)
Jones

Arthur
Harris

George Kahanu

O ne of the choice experiences that has come to me as a result of this book has been my privilege to meet others who were also at Pearl Harbor on December 7, 1941. There are many—too many to count, but among them are a naval pilot, a seaman, a marine bugler, a Honolulu policeman, a shipyard worker (my cousin who had never before told me what happened to him), and some of our neighbors from Pearl City, who happened to be Japanese-Americans. Along the way, I have learned that there are innumerable stories of December 7th, but I wanted to include just a few of them, as told to me by these new friends with whom I share a very special bond. Here are their stories . . .

Other Stories of the Pearl Harbor Attack
Arthur C. Harris, Honolulu Policeman

A rthur Harris is a large-framed man with huge hands and a powerful handshake. For many years he was a police officer, and even
though he is now 82 years old, it's easy to imagine him in the
brown uniform then worn by Honolulu police officers.

On Saturday, December 6, 1941, the fleet was in, which means that
most of the ships that were based in Pearl Harbor were in port, lined up
and anchored in their assigned locations. The ship crews had just gotten
paid, and had the weekend off. In those days, nearly all of the military
personnel were men, and they were in and around Honolulu looking for a
good time. Arthur was on duty that night, and he remembers the streets
being white with sailors, nicknamed "swabbies", plus lots of khaki uni-
forms (Army, Coast Guard and Marines) as well.

It was one of the busiest nights in Arthur's memory, because many of
the servicemen began drinking, and there were many calls to the police
department asking for help. Late that night, the servicemen, worn out from
partying, returned to their ships and fell asleep. Arthur remembers working until midnight, then headed for home.

Next morning, the Japanese attack began at 7:55, and at 8 o'clock,
when it was obvious that something terrible was happening, Arthur was
called back to duty. He reported to the main station, picked up a patrol car,
and headed toward Pearl City. On the road, he and his partner, Gene Burk,
could see smoke rising from the harbor. As they went along, Japanese
planes were strafing the road, so low they could see the pilots, and they

took cover under a bridge. Later, they were assigned to go to different areas because they had first aid equipment in the patrol car. In those days, there was no ambulance service in the rural areas of Oahu, so they acted as an ambulance as well as policemen. Can you imagine a police car being an ambulance?

As it grew dark, soldiers who were assigned to guard the electric transformers and reservoirs were "gun happy" and would shoot at anything that looked suspicious. They were even shooting out lights in homes because the island was supposed to be blacked out. Arthur took injured people to emergency hospitals, and the coroner's office was quickly filled with bodies. The scariest part was driving at night without any lights because of the blackout.

The night of December 7th, jittery gunners at Pearl Harbor shot down our own planes, thinking the Japanese had returned.

"That night, we shot down some of our own planes trying to land at Pearl Harbor. Our own gunners were knocking them down, there was so much confusion." For three days, Arthur didn't go home. He ate food on the run, "mooching" sandwiches wherever he could, and just kept going. There were only 250 policemen for the whole island, which was not nearly enough.

A lot of civilian casualties were caused by our own antiaircraft shells. The shells were supposed to explode in the air when they reached a certain altitude, but some of them didn't explode, and came back down and killed people who weren't even close to Pearl Harbor. A family named McCabe was killed by shells hitting their car while trying to get to their jobs in Pearl Harbor.

It was a terrible time, and Arthur thinks the Japanese could have taken the island if they had come in force. "They made a mistake by not destroying the shipyard repair shops in Pearl Harbor and the oil tanks which contained fuel for the military."

During the attack, all of our planes at nearby Wheeler Field were lined up in a row on the runway, and the Japanese planes came down and strafed them. Arthur remembers an army lieutenant named Welch, who wasn't at the field, but got in a car and drove there, and found a fighter plane that would still fly. He took off, and was able to knock down four Japanese planes.

People were so upset—their imaginations were running wild. There were all kinds of reports of paratroopers landing on beaches and out in the country, so Arthur spent hours chasing down rumors which turned out to be false. One report he especially remembers was of four paratroopers landing at a farm. It turned out to be cows grazing in a pasture!

"They say, being a policeman you shouldn't be afraid, 'cause you got a gun and a badge and everything, and should be fearless. But there's times when you kinda doubt whether you're fearless or not."

69

M.Sgt. Richard Fiske, Marine Corps bugler, USS *West Virginia*

"We were just talking like you and I are, and in the next second, we're in a world war. Just that quickly. It doesn't seem possible that one minute you're at peace, and the next minute, you're in a war."

I n 1993, we met Sgt. Richard Fiske on the grounds of the Arizona Memorial in Pearl Harbor. He was wearing his Pearl Harbor Survivors cap, and had a group of tourists around him. Since millions of visitors come to the Arizona Memorial from all over the world, we were not surprised that the people listening to him were from many countries, including Japan. He opened a thick notebook, and carefully turned its pages, showing photographs. We listened with fascination as he told his story with great warmth and sincerity.

Richard was a marine bugler, assigned to the battleship USS *West Virginia*, and on that Sunday morning, had just finished playing his bugle for the raising of the colors (American flag). It was just an ordinary day. He had the rest of the day off, and was looking forward to a date with a girlfriend in Honolulu.

But in the next few seconds, the world changed, and America was under attack. Richard was on the bridge of the *West Virginia*, which is high above the main deck, about 16 stories above the water. He had a ringside view as the Japanese torpedo planes suddenly attacked the side of his ship. They came in very low, only about 25 feet above the water, because the channel isn't very deep, and the torpedoes were specially designed for shallow water. (After the war, Richard met the man who designed those torpedoes, and learned that it took over two years to perfect them.)

After they released their torpedoes, the pilots would quickly climb and zoom past their target, looking back to see if they had been successful. The Japanese pilots had their cockpits open in case they needed to bail out, and Richard had a very close look at one of the pilots as his plane flew past, barely missing the bridge where Richard was standing in total shock and disbelief. Can you imagine how it must have felt to see that pilot roar by, and then to feel your ship rocked by torpedoes smashing into its side?

One torpedo was aimed wrong. It went too deep, and buried itself in the bottom over by the USS *Oklahoma*. It was found many years later, in May of 1991. It was still "alive", but was detonated and you can see the remains on display in the museum at the USS *Arizona* Memorial Visitor Center.

In his large notebook, Richard has a copy of a document from the War Historian in Tokyo, Japan. It is an official diagram of the attack plan in Japanese. It shows there were 40 torpedo planes, 49 high altitude bombers, 51 dive bombers and 43 fighters. The torpedoes were 18 feet long, and the USS *West Virginia* took nine of them.

His battleship was badly damaged, and had no water pressure to fight the fires that broke out on board. Fireboats came up and started spraying water on the fires. Richard left the bridge and joined his shipmates on deck, pouring buckets of sand on men whose clothes were on fire. Finally, the order came to abandon ship. Oil was leaking from the crippled ships, and the water was on fire as Richard and about 15 others dove off the *West Virginia*. They swam through the burning water toward Ford Island, which was about 60 yards away. He didn't know he could swim so fast!

Zenji Abe is one of the Japanese pilots who bombed the USS West Virginia. He and Richard Fiske have become good friends.

He and his buddies helped pull exhausted and wounded men out of the water as the second wave of planes came over. In addition to Captain Bennion, there were 106 men killed on the *West Virginia*, plus 375 wounded. The next day, Richard had the difficult task of playing taps for the burial of his captain.

Like many war veterans, Richard kept his story inside, and didn't talk about it for many years. The attack had filled him with hate for the Japanese, and he carried that hate with him until it ultimately made him sick. Finally, he told his story for the first time, and felt a release from the horror of his past.

In 1991, on the 50th anniversary of the attack, Richard met some of the Japanese pilots who had attacked his ship that day. In an incredible turn of events, time had softened feelings on both sides, healing began, and they have now become good friends. Once each month, on behalf of a Japanese pilot, Richard purchases two roses, one for the pilot and one for Richard, takes them to the Arizona Memorial, places the roses below the wall of names, and plays taps in a touching tribute to those who rest there. Those who hear him play will never forget it.

Once a month, Richard blows taps at the Arizona Memorial.

George Kahanu, welder in naval shipyard

George is my cousin, and yet it was only recently that I heard his Pearl Harbor story.

We tend to forget that civilians were in the harbor that day. George was a welder at that time, and was with a crew of men ready to go to work. But the welding supervisor had forgotten the keys to the "rod shack" where they kept the welding rods, and had to return to Honolulu to get them. So, the group of men sat down and began to talk about the football games from the night before.

Suddenly, they heard a series of loud BOOOMS! At first, they didn't think too much about it, because they were used to the Navy holding mock attacks. But it was Sunday morning, and they wondered why today? When the explosions continued, they decided to investigate. So they walked out of the shop and looked in the direction of Hickam airfield, where they could see huge clouds of very black smoke hanging in the sky above Hickam.

Above: In 1941, George Kahanu was a civilian employee of the Naval Shipyard in Pearl Harbor. Today, he is retired and lives on the island of Maui. Below: George could plainly see the "rising sun" insignia on the Japanese planes attacking the ships in Pearl Harbor.

They began to realize that something was wrong, but couldn't believe what they were seeing. They turned quickly, and saw torpedo bombers coming over the shop area, with the Japanese red meatball painted on the side. There were torpedoes hanging underneath the planes, and they could see the pilots clearly. They watched them circle and come around, then drop down to just above the water and drop their torpedoes.

In addition to the ships in Pearl Harbor, many American planes were destroyed, such as the B-17 above, and the fighter plane below, which never got off the ground.

They could see the splash, and then, several seconds later, the enormous explosion as a torpedo hit its mark. It was unbelievable, and they stood there for a few seconds, not knowing what to do. They looked at each other, and then a dive bomber attacked two cruisers in the dock across from them, the USS *St. Louis* and the USS *Honolulu*. That plane dropped a bomb and then began to strafe. George could see the bullets flying around them, and they came alive.

They ran to get back in the shop, but the door had been shut, and for a moment they couldn't get it open. Bullets were spraying everywhere as they fled to the side of the building, and then hit the ground, flat on their faces until the plane had passed. Then they scrambled up and hurried into the building for protection.

The first torpedo had hit the side of the USS *Oklahoma* battleship, followed by several more. In what seemed like about ten minutes, the *Oklahoma* rolled over on her port (left) side and went under. As they looked down the shipyard, other ships were exploding and burning.

They knew they had to do something to help, so they reported to the cruiser USS *San Francisco*, and began to install mounts for the anti aircraft guns. Previously, it would take about a week to install gun mounts for these big guns. But this time, under great pressure, it only took about an hour. Shortly afterward, the guns were firing, and from then on, they were ready.

The Japanese attack concentrated on destroying ships and planes. George says they missed the boat in not attacking the shops, which only had minor damage from flying shrapnel and stray bullets. If the shops had been wiped out, they would not have been able to repair the ships. This became a critical factor in the American war effort, because at least 15 of the ships that were damaged on December 7th, were repaired and returned to duty in the following months. George says, "There's no telling how the war might have turned out without the use of those ships."

When they checked the USS *Oklahoma* for damage, there were tapping sounds coming from the hull. So they knew there were people still alive, inside the ship, who couldn't get out because it was laying on its side, mostly below the surface.

Crews from George's shop brought pneumatic hammers to cut holes in the steel plating of the ship. George remembers that they saved quite a number of people by doing the tedious cutting nonstop until the hulls were opened. Risking their lives, divers went down into the submerged ships, trying to reach airtight compartments on the inside of the ship where men were trapped, while the shop crews were cutting from the outside. Sadly, in spite of their best efforts, not all of the trapped men were saved.

Millions of gallons of seawater were pumped from damaged and sunken ships before repairs could begin.

Above*: Repair crews swarm over a damaged ship, rushing to get it back in service. **Far Left:** The USS Oklahoma (foreground) capsized, trapping many crew members. Rescue teams cut through the steel hull while (**Left**) divers searched inside the ship to locate them.*

Our Neighbors in Pearl City—Americans of Japanese Ancestry

Our little community on the Pearl City Peninsula had an amazing variety of people and activities. There were fishermen, merchants, storekeepers, military officers and rice farmers, a small hotel, a yacht club, and most importantly for my family, the Pan American Clipper base where my mother worked.

Many of the families in our community were AJA's (Americans of Japanese ancestry). Earlier, thousands of Japanese men had come to Hawaii to work in the pineapple and sugar cane fields. In those days, it was the custom for those men to write back to their homes in search of wives. Photographs were exchanged, and in many cases, Japanese women came to the islands to be married. These women were called "picture brides."

Hazel and Tetsu Kobashigawa were daughters of a picture bride, and they lived only a few blocks from us. They were 15 and 14 years old, and remember December 7th very clearly.

"We were just getting up," said Tetsu. "It was a lazy Sunday," Hazel adds. "We heard all these sounds, we went out to the yard, and first thought it was military maneuvers."

Tetsu looks up, "And we said, my, they even put the red dots on the wings, you know, never thinking that it would be enemy planes. But when they started shooting, we took off."

"We turned the radio on, and that's when they said, 'This is the real McCoy.' My girlfriend and I got on our bikes, and we were gonna go

Hazel and Tetsu Kobashigawa, in Hazel's home above the Pearl City Peninsula, recall being evacuated from Pearl Harbor in a truck with other Japanese Americans.

Editor's Note: The Kobashigawa, Izawa and other Japanese-American families from Pearl City were among the last to receive an apology and payment from the United States (see page 52). Dorinda's brother, Ishmael Stagner, was instrumental in their long Reparation process.

down to the wharf and see what was happening. We were down by the park, and there were military men who told us to get back, get back. One of the neighbor kids came to our house on his bicycle, huffing and puffing, and told us all the ships were on fire."

"I don't think we were afraid at that time," says Hazel, "but when the military truck came by and told us, 'you can't take anything—get in the truck just as you are.' That's when we got scared."

"Then the truck went down the street, and got the other Japanese families from their homes—only the Japanese families. They took us up Waimano Home Road to a sugarcane field and told us, 'Don't move around, because you could get shot.' They took my brother away, and our Mom cried for weeks, not knowing where he was."

Shells and pieces of shrapnel picked up from her yard after the attack and saved by Tetsu Kobashigawa.

Hazel and Tetsu remember military guards being stationed at their evacuation site and not understanding why they (the Japanese families) were under suspicion as possible enemies. One day, their mother was allowed to go back to their home long enough to get some belongings, but a guard was constantly at her side.

"He had his bayonet, you know, at her back, and she was nervous—she couldn't even think of what she wanted to get. He's right there, to make sure she didn't get a hand grenade or something." Tetsu shakes her head and shudders at the memory.

Tetsu smiles, thinking back. "I took my dog, and my girlfriend took her dog, and nobody objected at that time, but when we were evacuated to

Thompson Izawa was fishing in Pearl Harbor when the attack began. Torpedo bombers flew directly over him on their way to attack U.S. ships.

Thompson and I chuckle over memories of living in Pearl City before the attack.

Waipahu, and they had to cook our food, they did object. Some of the people started complaining and saying, 'you better let the dogs go, because they are eating our food.' But I said, 'no, the food he is getting is from my share.' And that's how my friend and I were able to keep our dogs."

Over the next few days, many of the Pearl City residents were allowed to return to their homes. But not the Kobashigawa's and the other Japanese families. "We were not allowed to go back because we were Japanese," recalls Hazel, "It was a horrendous experience, going through something like that. But life goes on."

Another neighbor, Thompson Izawa, was from another Japanese family in Pearl City. He and his father had gotten up at 5:00 a.m. on December 7th to go fishing and were out in the water when the first Japanese planes bombed the USS *Utah* directly in front of them. Thompson tells his story:

"During the attack, we saw a torpedo bomber come right overhead—with a long torpedo. We were out in the water, fishing, and that torpedo landed only a few hundred feet away. It hit the *Utah*, and that one torpedo capsized it. Later, I found out that people inside the engine room were pounding on the hull, and when others heard that sound, they cut that thing open, and a lot of people survived.

"I wish I had a machine gun—I could have shot some of those planes down—seriously! They were so low, especially the torpedo bombers. They came over the Waianae range like bees and all hell broke loose. At first, I thought they were making a movie. But when my Dad saw the torpedoes and the insignia on the wings, that's when he grabbed me by the ear and we took off, and went back home, you know. All the neighbors, the Japanese neighbors, were at my home. It was easy for the military to pick us up, because we were all together at our house. They put us in a truck and hauled us all to the mountains and left us there under guard. They had fixed bayonets, the security guards.

"We stayed in the mountains, and kept together. It rained overnight, and the following day they transported us to Waipahu, and we stayed there two to three weeks. We ate rice balls, and they brought us blankets and pillows. We slept on the floor. We survived, that's the main thing, we survived. Several days after the attack, non-Japanese people were allowed to go home. We were not. They searched our home, and they found a 12 gauge shotgun. My Dad used it to scare birds away from the rice fields. They took that away.

"Later, I learned that the Army had picked up the Japanese planes on radar when they were still coming in, but somehow they mistook them for American B-17's coming in from California. I never could understand—the approaching planes were coming from the north. How could the B-17's come from the north? But they didn't figure that out, and that's why a terrible thing happened. It was a surprise, and we couldn't fight back.

"It was disastrous—I never want to see that sight again!"

When I asked Thompson if there was ever any question of whether his family felt Japanese or American, his answer was firm.

"Never! It was never a question for us—we were absolutely Americans! We were loyal!"

Thompson and I search for the ruins of the Palm Lodge, where an American pilot was killed by "Friendly Fire" on the night of December 7, 1941.

Melvin E. Jones (Jonesie), Navy barber aboard USS *Nevada*

"Who do you think started the officer's barber shop In Pearl Harbor? I did. I went to downtown Honolulu, bought 9 dollars worth of supplies. I operated it for three months, then sold it for 8 dollars, so it cost me one dollar. At that time, it was 24 cents for a haircut, 20 cents for a shave."

When you realize that a battleship is really a floating city, you understand the need for lots of specialized skills that are needed for the city to operate properly. Melvin E. Jones has a special skill that is needed on a battleship with a couple of thousand men on board—he's a barber!

On Sunday morning, December 7, 1941, Jonesie was in his barber shop on board the USS *Nevada*, anchored in Pearl Harbor. The *Nevada* was first in a line of battleships that was aptly called, "Battleship Row", which was to become the primary target of the Japanese attack.

But Jonesie was unaware of all that. He was sitting in his barber's chair enjoying his coffee and reading the newspaper. Suddenly he heard something that sounded like firecrackers. Somebody ran across his shop to a porthole, and looked out to see planes with red circles on their wings and body.

Jonesie doesn't remember what happened to the newspaper and coffee—he just bolted out the door and up a ladder to the main deck aft and looked up. The sky was filled with planes that swarmed over Ford Island like flies over a piece of cake. He saw one torpedo plane after another, flying very low just above the water. One of them peeled off past the stern, and *Nevada's* gunners tracked him across with a 50 caliber machine gun and brought him down. That plane exploded with the bluest cloud of smoke that Jonesie had ever seen.

On a battleship, every crew member has a battle station, even a barber. So, under enemy attack—what does a barber do? Well, he goes to his battle station, and that's what Jonesie did, on the double.

The *Nevada* attempted to get underway, to move out of its mooring. Jonesie skidded down a ladder to where the ship was tied up, and helped get the huge mooring lines off. He wished for an ax to cut them, but there was none. Meantime, the USS *Arizona* had exploded, releasing clouds of dark smoke that made it difficult to even see what they were doing. They struggled until they were finally able to raise the mooring lines enough to release the ship.

The USS Nevada was at the head of the line of ships called, "Battleship Row." To avoid blocking the harbor channel, the badly damaged Nevada attempts to run itself aground.

He saw sailors in the water, which had patches of fire everywhere. They would come up for air, then go back down and try to swim underneath the fire to get as far away as possible.

Jonesie remembers seventeen planes dive bombing his ship, with five of them hitting their target. He went below, into a watertight compartment that was suddenly filled with smoke so black you couldn't see your hand in front of you. He was knocked flat by a jolt when more bombs hit, and felt like a rat in a hole with no way out. In the darkness, he found an oily rag and shoved his face in it trying to breathe. After awhile, the smoke was pumped from the room, and it cleared up so he could see again.

The ship was shuddering, and Jonesie wasn't sure if the ship was underway or beached. He was still below deck when water began to come in. They'd evacuate one compartment, then move to the next, passing ammunition through a hatch. Then, somebody's feet came through. Jonesie grabbed the feet and helped lift him into the compartment. The man had a gas mask on, but in the crisis had forgotten to pull the retainer tape off the cannister, and he had suffocated to death.

When the attack finally ended, Jonesie made his way up on deck, where he saw row after row of dead crew members, wrapped in dirty blankets. In those days, brothers were allowed to be on the same ship. Jonesie remembers one seaman who couldn't find his brother, and went hurriedly from body to body, pulling the blankets back to see who it was, hoping he wouldn't find his brother. Today, Navy regulations don't allow brothers to serve on the same ship.

Above: Jonesie still cuts hair in his barber shop in Marshall, Missouri that is filled with pictures and souvenirs. Below: My husband, Larry, gets a trim from the former officer's barber from the USS Nevada.

Finally, Jonesie told me, "It was a terrible thing, and should never be forgotten. I'm lucky to be here at eighty three and one half."

Captain Jim Daniels, Fighting Squadron Six, U.S. Navy, based on the USS *Enterprise*

I met Captain Jim Daniels at Pearl Harbor, where we were both speakers at a commemorative event for the 50th anniversary of the bombing in 1991. I was there to represent the civilian story and the children of WWII in Hawaii. He was there to tell his remarkable story of Fighting Squadron Six from the aircraft carrier, USS *Enterprise*.

Young Ensign Daniels was a pilot on the *Enterprise*, due into Pearl Harbor the night of December 6th. But a winter storm delayed them at sea. If the *Enterprise* had made it in, she would have been anchored next to the battleship USS *Utah*, which was sunk during the bombing. So the fateful storm saved the *Enterprise* from the Japanese attack, which was most fortunate.

The *Enterprise* was navigating through heavy seas, about 125 miles southwest of Hawaii when it received a wire announcing the Japanese attack. Admiral Halsey, on the *Enterprise*, decided to send his own dive bombers, torpedo planes and fighters to find the Japanese fleet. Jim Daniels was second in command of the fighter group, and they searched for hours, but did not find their target.

When they returned to the *Enterprise*, it was dark, and they requested permission to land aboard the carrier. Halsey, not knowing where the Japanese submarines were, made a difficult decision. He refused to light up the deck to bring them in, fearing they might be spotted by Japanese submarines. He knew how important his ship had now become, and was unwilling to take the risk. So he ordered the fighter planes to go to Pearl

U. S. FLEET
COMM. ..NDER AIRCRAFT, BATTLE

G: OOTH V 2GHF Z FSL 071830 CBQ TART O BT

URGENT   URGENT

AIR RAID ON PEARL HARBOR X THIS IS NOT DRILL.

Top: Daniels is now retired from the navy.
Middle: Looking back after a carrier takeoff.
Bottom: The telegram received on the USS *Enterprise* announcing the Japanese attack.

Above: Planes line up for takeoff from the USS Enterprise. Below: Marines "dig in" at Pearl Harbor. Later, virtually every gun in the area shot at Jim's squadron when they tried to land at night on Ford Island.

Harbor. But he had to allow the torpedo planes to land, because they were out of gas. This was extremely dangerous, because they still had their torpedoes, and it was the first time torpedo planes with loaded torpedoes had landed on a carrier at night.

Meanwhile, Jim's group of six fighters turned and headed for Pearl Harbor with no lights and no communication. They flew in the darkness, one above the other, so they could look from one cockpit down to the next. Their engine exhaust manifolds were white hot and their instrument panel lights were red. They lined up and kept this formation all the way back to Pearl Harbor. As they pushed on through the black skies, their fuel gauges dropped closer and closer to the empty mark.

But after a masterful job of navigation, Jim's squadron hit Barber's Point on the nose. They contacted the airfield tower at Ford Island for permission to land. And then, just as they broke from their formation to land, every gun in the area opened up on them. It was Americans shooting at Americans. The gunners on the ground were "trigger happy" from the Japanese attack earlier that day, and assumed that the Japanese had returned. They didn't wait to find out who these planes were up there in the darkness. One gunner shot, and that's all it took for everyone with a weapon to open fire against the six planes in Jim's squadron.

Jim said the shells and bullets and tracers were "so thick you could walk on it," and Jim's squadron was nearly wiped out. The #1 plane (Fritz Hebel) went down at Wheeler field, #2 (Herb Mengus) crashed at Pearl City. #3 (Gale Herman) crashed on Ford Island, but he managed to walk away. The #4 pilot (Davey Flynn) bailed out; they thought he was a Japanese paratrooper and shot him as he landed. Jim Daniels was #5, and he flew past and circled out for another attempt. The #6 pilot (Eric Allen) bailed out over the tower, and was shot in the chest with a 50 caliber machine gun, and died about 2 a.m. the next morning.

Jim Daniels was still in the air, and still being shot at as he came back around. He was talking to the tower and they gave permission to land. He rolled his wheels down and hit his flaps. He should have landed at 85 knots, but landed much faster, at 120 knots. He managed to get his plane stopped, and then taxied back to their hanger. There was a marine with a machine gun, who started to shoot at Jim, with bullets flying just over his head. Gale Herman, who had just reached the ground, hit the marine with the butt of a rifle and quieted him down.

With great emotion, Jim described what had happened. "You're so intent on doing everything right and getting the plane down. You are so well trained—you do everything exactly as you were trained, and if you do that, you'll live. If you don't, if you make a mistake, then you're dead."

"All I knew was, there's the field, and I had to get down. I didn't have any gas. My wheels were down, but I didn't know if they locked. I must have done everything right, and obviously I did. It's a terrible experience to be shot at by your own people. Of the six planes from the Enterprise, five planes were shot down by friendly fire, three of us were killed, and one died later. I'm the only guy alive that got an airplane down that night safely."

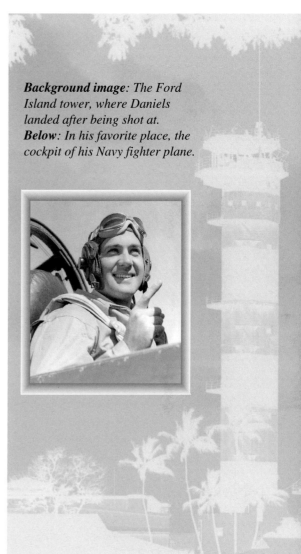

Background image: The Ford Island tower, where Daniels landed after being shot at.
Below: In his favorite place, the cockpit of his Navy fighter plane.

After the attack, we spent several nights sleeping on the floor in the recreation hall at the Waipahu Sugar Mill.

When the military police wouldn't let us return to our home on the peninsula, we hid up here in the sugarcane fields.

After the war, the Navy took over the entire Pearl City Peninsula, and we moved here to Halawa.

Pearl City Police station, where Arthur Harris reported for duty.

Alongside this road, we watched the burning battleships from our '39 Ford.

Waipahu

Pearl City Peninsula

Pearl Harbor

USS Utah

USS Arizona

USS Nevada, where seaman Melvin Jones (Jonesie) was aboard

The Pan American Clipper base, where my Mom worked.

Ford Island

Battleship Row

USS West Virginia, where Marine Sgt. Richard Fiske was stationed

Waipio Point

Shipyard dock area, where George Kahanu was working on the day of the attack

Ford Island runway, where Capt. Jim Daniels managed to land his fighter after flying through a storm of "friendly fire" from our own American forces

N

Our front yard is where we first saw the Japanese planes fly directly over our heads on their way to attack Pearl Harbor. This photo was taken later, after we had been issued our gas masks.

Pacific

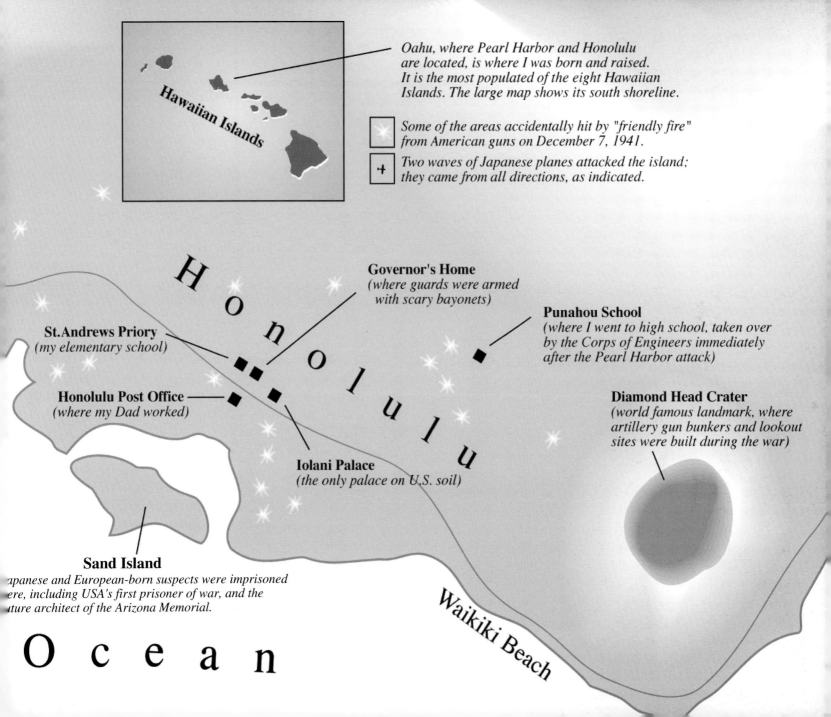

Oahu, where Pearl Harbor and Honolulu are located, is where I was born and raised. It is the most populated of the eight Hawaiian Islands. The large map shows its south shoreline.

Hawaiian Islands

Some of the areas accidentally hit by "friendly fire" from American guns on December 7, 1941.

Two waves of Japanese planes attacked the island; they came from all directions, as indicated.

H o n o l u l u

Governor's Home
(where guards were armed with scary bayonets)

Punahou School
(where I went to high school, taken over by the Corps of Engineers immediately after the Pearl Harbor attack)

St.Andrews Priory
(my elementary school)

Honolulu Post Office
(where my Dad worked)

Iolani Palace
(the only palace on U.S. soil)

Diamond Head Crater
(world famous landmark, where artillery gun bunkers and lookout sites were built during the war)

Sand Island
apanese and European-born suspects were imprisoned ere, including USA's first prisoner of war, and the ature architect of the Arizona Memorial.

Waikiki Beach

O c e a n

Postscript

Dad and I, pictured in 1991 at his apartment near Kansas City, where we prepared the anniversary talks we would give in Hawaii on December 7th of that year. Dad died July 8, 1995.

Each time I return to Hawaii, I rush down to the Pearl City Peninsula hoping that the old pier and Pan American marker are still there. The Navy continues to control the area, which is now filled with military housing that has disguised the land so much that it's hard to find the original streets. Just about everything else is gone, but the memories and emotions are still there as I walk along the harbor.

Another generation of children now plays there, completely unaware of the history surrounding them. Not only do I wish they knew the Pearl Harbor story, I wish that all American school children knew this part of their American history—where a war was fought on American soil. Including the stories of Daniels, Harris, Fiske, Jones, Kahanu, and my Pearl City neighbors is an attempt to make other Pearl Harbor stories more accessible to American students. I am grateful to these people for being so generous in allowing me to add dimension to what happened on that date of infamy.

With the USS *Missouri* moored at its new home in Pearl Harbor, perhaps there will be renewed interest in the Pearl Harbor story. Somehow, it seems fitting for the ship that marked the end of WWII, to find a home in Pearl Harbor next to the USS *Arizona* Memorial, where the war began. Your interest in this most significant part of American history is humbly appreciated. I thank you for letting me share a child's view of the Pearl Harbor story.

My aloha to you.

Dorinda Makanaonalani Nicholson

USS Arizona Memorial

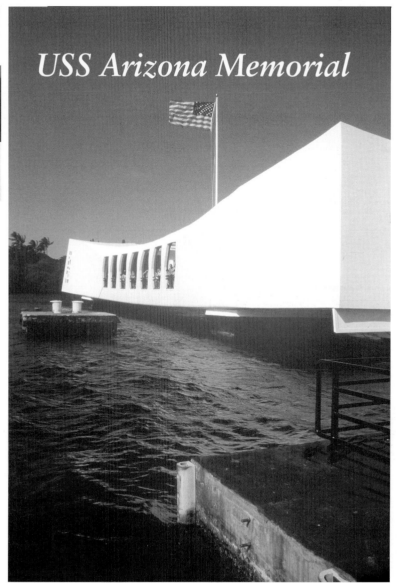

Finally, I want to say something about the beautiful Arizona Memorial in Pearl Harbor. As with many other things we've described in this book, there is an ironic story about this structure. It was designed by a man named Alfred Preis, who grew up in Austria, earning a degree in architecture. He had a dream of coming to America, and specifically to Hawaii. He arrived in Hawaii in 1939 with the promise of a job as a designer, which he took. But on the day after the Pearl Harbor attack, he was taken into custody along with other Europeans, moved to an internment camp at Sand Island, and held there for over a year. Finally, he was paroled, and allowed to remain in Hawaii. He became a naturalized citizen in 1946, and later began his affiliation with the Arizona Memorial, ending with his selection as its architect. How remarkable that a man who was held prisoner at Sand Island should be selected to create a monument that inspires great feeling and emotions, and achieves his design goal of permitting "the individual to contemplate his own personal response . . . his innermost feelings."

I am very proud that this book was made possible by the Arizona Memorial Museum Association.

D.M.N.

References

Knudsen, Eric A. TELLER OF HAWAIIAN TALES, 1945, published by Coca-Cola Bottling Company, Honolulu, T.H. (out of print)

Credits—Photographs, illustrations, props

Author's Collection—Cover, Title Page, Dedication, 11, 12, 19, 26, 27, 35, 37T, 55T, 59, 61

Bishop Museum—29L, 47

DeSoto Brown Collection—39, 40

Jim Daniels Collection—81, 83M, 83B, 84T, 85 (inset)

Abel L. Dolim Collection—13, 14, 20, 38

Ken Hatfield, Lee's Summit Journal—88

Hawai'i State Archives—32T

Senator Daniel K. Inouye—52, 53

Johnson County Museum System—15, 36, 46, 49B, 50

Rita Klepac—41

National Archives—64T, 68, 71, 73B, 74, 75, 81, 84B

National Archives/Central Plains—44L, 48

Larry Nicholson—7-10, 16, 21, 22, 25, 29, 46, 55B, 59, 60, 62, 63, 64B, 65-67, 69, 70, 72, 73T, 76-80, 82, 83T, 86-87, 89-90, Inside back cover

Harry S. Truman Library—57, 58

University of Hawai'i War Records Depository—24B, 30T, 30B, 33L, 34, 37B, 43, 44R, 45, 54, 56T, 56B

US Army—42

US Army Museum of Hawai'i—32B, 51

USS *Arizona* Memorial Photo Archives, National Park Service—12T, 17, 18, 23, 28T, 28B, 31, 33R, 71, 73, 81, 84

Jim Wilbert Collection—49T